The Awesome

FOR YOUNG FILMAKERS

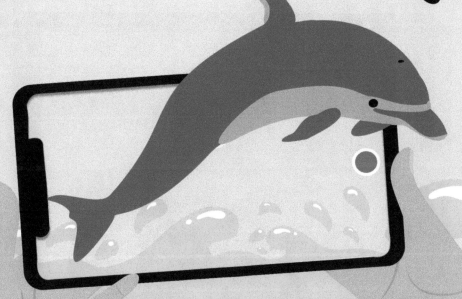

By Mike Murphy, MEd

The Awesome Companion Book
FOR YOUNG FILMAKERS

By Mike Murphy, MEd

Companion Books

A Division of

Retro Ranger
Publishing Company

Awesome Companion Books
a division of
Retro Ranger Publishing Company
Oshkosh, WI.

To all young graphic artists, designers, musicians, writers, movie makers, and performers who have constantly amazed me through the years. I hope you have the opportunity to continue to express yourselves and sparkle the world with your imagination.

Mike M.

Table of Contents

What is an Awesome Companion Book

The Awesome Companion Books are a series of "How To" guides for adults and children. Each book in the series has a companion book designed for young people. The books can be used independently or in concert with its companion book.

The Awesome Companion Books have crossover activities to engage both older and younger movie makers.

Look for the clapboard symbol to indicate a companion activity.

This book is designed for young people to understand and practice the basics of video recording. The companion to this book is The Awesome Companion Book of Home Movie Making where family and friends can explore more advanced movie making skills.

All books in this series emphasize collaboration, cooperation, companionship and fun. Enjoy.

Anyone can record a video with their smartphone, but making a good video is more of a challenge. Creating a professional looking recording of a parade, a baseball game, a pet show or 4th of July fireworks requires some knowledge and practice of recording techniques. Understanding some of the basics of good video recording will help you create better videos.

This book will show you the proper techniques for using a smartphone for video recording. A smartphone or smart device is like an entire video production studio that you can hold in your hand, which, if you think about it, is pretty amazing. With the right apps you can record video, edit video, add titles, add music and then share it on your favorite social media platform all on a smartphone. With the help of this book and your own imagination, let's go out and make some great videos!

What can you do with a video camera

Record a school play.

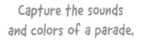

Capture the sounds and colors of a parade.

Write and produce your own movie

Record yourself playing a musical instrument

Create a video series of you demonstrating your favorite hobby and post it on-line.

Create a video memory of your family picnic or gathering

Document nature in your backyard or a park

How a Smartphone Works

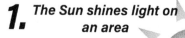
1. The Sun shines light on an area

2. The camera lens sees the image.

3. The image is captured by a sensor chip inside the camera,

4. The sensor turns the image into an electrical signal.

5. The camera takes the electrical signal and turns it into an image or video.

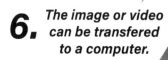

6. The image or video can be transferred to a computer.

Using Smartphones

In addition to all the other features a smartphone has to offer, it contains a very high quality camera. The camera on a smartphone can record very high definition video that, in the past, would have required expensive and bulky equipment. In fact, major movies and commercials have been recorded using just a smartphone.

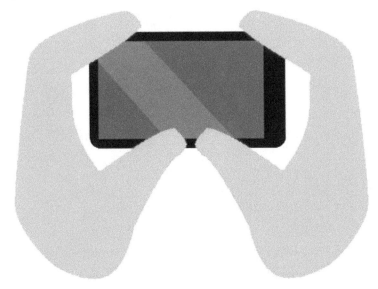

Holding a Smartphone for Recording

The best way to hold the smart phone is horizontally otherwise known as "landscape" position. TV's and computer screens all are designed for landscape images so your video should fill the screen or frame of your smartphone. What is a frame? What you see on the screen of your smart phone is your video frame. What you can fit in the frame is what you will record. So make sure your subject fits in the frame before recording.

The Red Button

When you hold up your smartphone to capture a moment, make sure you are actually recording video. It sounds silly but you'd be surprised how many people think they are recording something special only to get home and realize they forgot to press the record button. So don't forget. Press the red button on the smartphone camera app and make sure the numbers on the screen are advancing.

Also, before you start recording, check to see how much storage space you have available on your smartphone. One hour of record time takes up about 10GB of space. You should be able to check the amount of storage space available in the settings feature of your smart device.

Keep It Clean

Before you start recording with your smartphone, make sure that the camera lens is clean. Dust and smudges on the camera lens can show up in your recording and ruin a good video.

The best and safest way to clean the camera lens is to use a lint free cloth. You can purchase these cloths at most department stores. Never use facial tissue or paper towel. These are wood products that can actually scratch and leave small flecks of dust on the lens.

Gently rub the lens in a circle pattern. Also, clean the front (selfie) camera lens and the flash/light next to the back camera

Focus

To avoid blurry or fuzzy video, you need to focus your camera. Focusing refers to adjusting the camera so that the image is sharp and clean. For smartphones, you use the touch screen.

Once you have the subject in your frame, touch the center of the screen. A "box" should appear. This tells the camera to focus wherever you touch the screen. If you wanted the background in focus but not the subject, you would touch the screen where the background appears.

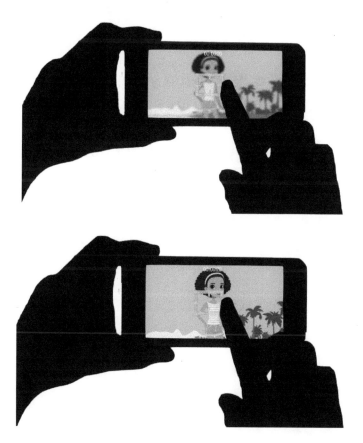

Keep Camera Steady

ŀ
s
y
ɑ
y
t
ʋ

mendations to prevent your
m shaking and moving when
rding. Stand or sit up straight
r arms and elbows close to
eath slowly so you don't shake
hone. Hold your smart phone
nds for a steady video.

er possible, lean against
g to take the weight off your
legs. It can be a tree, a chair, your friend or whatever is around. Sometimes sitting down instead of standing helps to stop the shakiness.

Tripods are a great way to keep your camera steady while you are recording. Tripods are three legged support systems for holding cameras. There is more information about tripods later in the book.

To stop camera shakiness, brace against
a tree, a building, a telephone pole, a car
(that's not moving), anything that will take
the weight off your legs so you don't rock
back and forth.

Heel to Toe

To create the effect of the camera moving toward a subject, walk slowly heel to toe. Hold the camera with your arms in toward your body and walk in long strides instead of quick steps.

Using a tripod for a steady video

"Was there an earthquake while you were recording this?"

Lighting is Important

It is important to take control of light when recording video. Avoid recording facing a bright light or in front of a window on a sunny day. The person will look very dark because the smart phone is trying to adjust for the outside light. Instead have the person face the window to take advantage of the bright sunlight.

LIGHTING TIPS

If you are recording inside and it appears dark, turn on some lights. You may have to adjust the lights to

Image by Jerzy Górecki from Pixabay

avoid casting dark shadows behind the subject. If necessary, bounce the lights off a white ceiling or tape some white paper to a sheet of cardboard and reflect the light on your subject.

Composition

Composition refers to how the subject is placed in the camera frame. Videographers, artists, and photographers practice composition techniques

when creating art, images or video. Understanding some simple composition rules will help you make better looking videos.

One guide is called "The Rule of Thirds". Imagine there are four lines in a tic- tac- toe pattern placed over the image on your smartphone screen. Most smartphones have a grid option that you can turn on to help you place the main subject where the lines cross. If the subject is a person or animal facing right, place it where the lines cross on the left and vice versa. This often is a better alternative then just placing the subject in the middle of the screen.

The Awesome Companion Book for Junior Movie Makers

Image by Predrag Kezic from Pixabay

In the example above, the lines intersect on the panda's head and body on the left of the screen. Below, the lines intersect over the orangutan on the right side of the screen

Image by Mike Murphy

Headroom

Headroom is the space between the top of the subject and the top of the frame. Avoid too little or too much headroom when framing your subject.

Too little headroom

Too much headroom

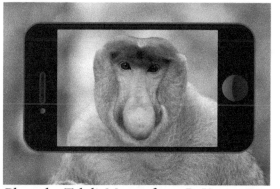

Correct headroom

Photo by TakdirMappe from PxHere

Nose room

Nose room is the space between the subject's nose and the edge of the smartphone screen. When framing your subject from the side avoid having too much nose room or too little nose room.

Anticipate Action

If the subject you are recording is moving, like a car or players in a soccer game, always leave a little space in front of the object so the viewer can anticipate the direction of the action.

Image by Sebastian Del Val from Pixabay

Image by LaBruixa from Pixabay

What is a Shot?

Movies and videos are made up of a series of shots. A shot is defined as a single, continuous operation of the camera. In other words, whenever you start recording and then stop recording you've created a shot.

In the very early days, movies were just one shot of people performing in front of the camera like a stage play. Now, films are much more sophisticated. Today movies are a combination of hundreds of shots organized in a specific order to tell a story. For each individual shot, the camera often changes position or location. See if you can identify the number of shots in a short video, or commercial.

   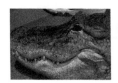

Each of these video segments represent a "shot" from the documentary video "Wisconsin Pet Expo".

Framing Terms

Movie makers and videographers use terms that describe the placement of the subject in your camera frame. These terms refer to the distance and angle of the camera to the subject. This is known as framing a shot. If a movie director tells the camera operator to record a distant or wide shot of a group of people, the camera operator has a general idea of how to place the camera.

You can learn more about movie making with the Awesome Companion Book of Home Movie Making.

Example of a Wide Shot

Example of a Close Up Shot

The Awesome Companion Book for Junior Movie Makers

Extreme Wide Shot

Wide Shot

Medium Wide Shot

Medium Shot

Close Up

High Angle

Low Angle

Eye Level

High Angle
Looking Down Above the Subject

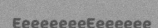

Eeeeeeeee Eeeeeeee

Eye Level
Recording at the subject's eye height

Low Angle
Looking Up Below the Subject

The Awesome Companion Book for Junior Movie Makers

Panning

A pan refers to the horizontal movement of the camera. Panning is a great method to cover a large area in one shot. The best way to record a pan is to mount your camera to a tripod, then start recording with the camera pointed all the way to the left or right and slowly move to the opposite side.

If you don't have a tripod, then hold the camera steady and place your feet on the ground facing forward. Move the upper part of your body left or right without moving your feet.

Practice panning around the living room, a park, your backyard, city street or large row of flowers. Move the camera slow and steady and don't rush. A fast pan is hard to watch on video.

Dolly

A dolly shot is when you move the camera toward or away from your subject within a single shot. A dolly refers to a wheeled cart or a cart on rails like a train. The camera person sits on the cart and is pushed or pulled by a production assistant. If you don't have a cart or a wagon then your legs will act as your dolly.

Using a dolly is great for a "point of view" shot where the camera acts as the eyes of the viewer. It makes the viewer feel as if they are a part of the action. Try using the dolly shot to walk up to a door of a house or walk toward a group of people talking, or down a long corridor and opening a mysterious door at the end.

When moving the camera forward or backward, hold your camera with your elbows close to your body and walk heel to toe. Practice several times until you can record a steady and smooth dolly shot.

Sit and Spin

Another technique to capture a large area is a 360° sit and spin. Using a swivel chair or stool, have someone slowly spin you in a complete circle while you are recording with a smartphone. Be careful. If you spin too fast you might make your viewers dizzy.

Many Shots Sarah

If you are out recording at an event or a special location such as a zoo, don't be a "One Shot Sam". Sam records a single shot from one point of view and moves on. Be a "Many Shots Sarah" and record multiple shots of your subject at different angles, heights and distances. Your video will be more engaging and interesting.

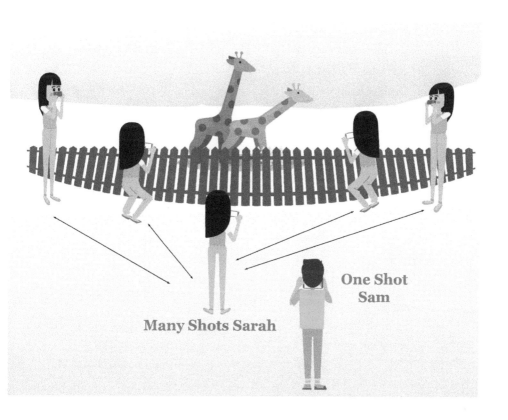

One Shot Sam

Many Shots Sarah

Projects

Here are some fun activities that you can do with the smartphone video camera. For some of these projects, you may need the help of a family member or friend.

Project #1 - Different Views

A. Did you ever imagine how a dog sees the world? Here's an excellent way to find out. Bring the smart phone down low where a dog's eye would be and record your surroundings for a brand new outlook.

B. Lay on your back and record looking up at the world. Try recording underneath a tree with the leaves moving in the wind or statues in the park. Have your friends gather around you looking down and singing a song.

The Awesome Companion Book for Junior Movie Makers

Project #2 - A Moving Video

Have someone pull or push you slowly in a wagon or cart or even a wheel chair while you are recording. This is called a tracking shot. A tracking shot is similar to a dolly shot except this time your are moving alongside or parallel to the action. Tracking shots are most often used to cover a large area in just shot.

When using a tracking shot, hold the smartphone steady and try not to tilt it left or right. If you are in a car you could hold your camera up against the window area to record the landscape rushing by.

This is great!
Just one more time around the park.

Project #3 - Interviewing

News programs, talk shows and documentary movies often consist of people discussing real life events or voicing their opinions on various topics. These question and answer sessions are known as interviews.

Video recording interviews with family and friends is a great way to keep a historical record of stories and memories.

You can ask your parents or grandparents about growing up when they were young. Ask your friend to tell you what they like about school or discuss their favorite hobby. One great interviewing technique is to have the person show pictures and objects that hold special memories. You'd be surprised at how much you can learn and share.

Setting Up the Interview

Have the person you are interviewing sit in a comfortable chair or across a table. It is very difficult to hold the camera steady while asking questions. Instead mount your smartphone on a tripod. A tripod is a three legged support system for cameras. You will also need a smart phone tripod mount. You attach the smartphone holder to a tripod and then the smartphone to the holder.

There are two basic types of tripods. The floor tripod that can reach up to six feet or more, and tabletop or mini tripods. The mini tripods are great when interviewing someone from across a table or desk.

Interviewing Tips

Find a quiet room for recording

Keep the camera in a horizontal position

Adjust camera for proper headroom

Place the camera close to you at eye level so the interviewee looks into the camera when answering your wquestions.

Make sure the interviewee is well lit and not sitting in front of a window.

Use a regular tripod or desktop tripod with asmartphone adapter or prop the camra up using a hommade stand

Listen to the person your are interviewing and ask more questions based on their answers

SAMPLE INTERVIEW QUESTIONS

 What's your favorite subject in school and why?

(to an adult) what was it like going to school when you were young?

 What is your favorite kind of music? Why?

What is your favorite tv show? Why?

 If you could meet anyone in history who would it be and why?

If you could go anywhere in the world where would you go and why?

Project #4 - Events

A gathering of family and friends for the holidays, a birthday party, or a picnic, is a great opportunity to grab the smartphone and start recording. Creating video memories is a wonderful gift to share.

Good movies aren't just a random collection of shots put together in no specific order. Instead, whether it is a get together, the zoo, a carnival, or a parade, your goal is to tell a story with your camera. Remember, all good movies, like good stories, have a beginning, middle and end.

Before you grab the camera and start recording, think about what kind of story you want to tell. Write down the type of video shots you want to include in your story. Good preparation equals great video.

There is more about how to put all your shots into a single movie in *The Awesome Companion Book of Home Movie Making*.

Video Checklist

✓ Outdoor clothes

✓ Check iPhone storage capacity

✓ Check iPhone battery level

✓ Tripod (if needed)

✓ Smartphone tripod mount (if needed)

✓ Clean camera lens

What is the subject of your video?

Motorcycle races

Where are you recording?

Elkhorn Wisconsin Race Track

What story do you want to tell with your video?

Show what it's like to be at the motorcycle races.

List of shots you will need

Wide shot of race area	Racers preparing their bikes
Shots of spectators gathering near the race track	Shots of the different motorcycles
Short interviews with some of the racers	Shots of motorcycles lining up at the starting area
Shots of the flag as the race begins	Shots of motorcycles racing on the track.
Shots of the motorcycle wheels as the race by.	Shots of spectators cheering
Shots of the winning racers	Final shots leaving the race track

Reminders

Try not to record into the sun or a bright light

Hold smartphone horizontally when recording

Walk steadily and smoothly

Get down to the level of your subject when possible.

Watch the focus of the camera.

Keep the camera level.

Video Checklist

☐ Outdoor clothes

☐ Check iPhone storage capacity

☐ Check iPhone battery level

☐ Tripod (if needed)

☐ Smartphone tripod mount (if needed)

☐ Clean camera lens

What is the subject of your video?

Where are you recording?

What story do you want to tell with your video?

List of shots you will need

Reminders

Try not to record into the sun or a bright light
Hold smartphone horizontally when recording
Walk steadily and smoothly
Get down to the level of your subject when possible.
Watch the focus of the camera.
Keep the camera level.

The Awesome Companion Book for Junior Movie Makers

Video Checklist

You can download and print additional Video Checklists at the URL below or scan the QR code for access to the web page.

https://www.retrorangerpub.com/video-checklist

What Makes a Good Story?

SETTING
The time and place of the action

Hiking trail near the mountains

CHARACTERS
Who is doing the action

Group of hikers

PLOT
What happens in the story

Hikers need to get to base camp before nightfall

THEME
What is the meaning of the story

Learning to overcome obstacles and working together

CONFLICT
What problem does the character need to solve?

Hiking around the mountain

Trip to the Zoo
Planning Guide

☐ Get a wide shot of the entrance to show the audience where everything takes place.

☐ Shots of people reading the programs and the zoo maps

☐ A pan of the zoo area.

☐ Wide shots, medium shots and close ups of animals.

☐ Shots of the information signs for each animal you record.

☐ Shots of family and friends enjoying the zoo.

☐ Moving shots on the Zoo trolley or train.

☐ Ask a zookeeper or employee to talk about the zoo or specific animals

☐ Shot of everyone leaving the zoo

Project #5 - Nature

Nature is a great subject for a video. Rivers flowing, wind rustling through trees, bees pollinating flowers,

squirrels and chipmunks looking for food, birds on the ground and in the air, all are great opportunities to take out the smartphone and start recording.

You can experience nature all year round and in all kinds of locations. Depending on where you live, you should try and capture all four seasons. Life emerging in spring. Nature at its liveliest in summer. All the colors in fall and the animal tracks revealed in the new fallen snow of winter.

You don't have to go to a park or nature preserve to experience nature. Check your own backyard or walk around your neighborhood. Nature is present everywhere.

RECORDING NATURE

BE PATIENT. SOMETIMES YOU HAVE TO WAIT TO GET A GOOD SHOT OF ANIMALS. IF YOU SEE A BIRD TO RECORD, STAY STILL AND QUIETLY POINT YOUR CAMERA. IF YOU HAVE A BIRD FEEDER IN YOUR YARD YOU MIGHT HAVE TO DO SOME CAMOUFLAGE WORK IN ORDER TO HIDE YOU AND YOUR CAMERA FROM THE BIRDS.

WALK QUIETLY THROUGH THE PARK OR THE WOODS SO THE WILDLIFE ISN'T SCARED OFF.

GET DOWN TO THE LEVEL OF YOUR SUBJECT. IF YOU SEE SOME INTERESTING LOOKING INSECTS ON THE GROUND OR ON A FLOWER, TRY AND KNEEL DOWN AND RECORD AT ITS LEVEL.

USE MOVING SHOTS. IF YOU ARE RECORDING LEAVES FALLING FROM THE TREES IN FALL, SLOWLY AND STEADILY MOVE THE CAMERA FROM ACROSS THE TREES. REMEMBER, VIDEO, UNLIKE PHOTOGRAPHY, REQUIRES MOVEMENT, EITHER ON YOUR PART OR OF THE SUBJECT YOU ARE RECORDING.

SHOOT FROM VARIOUS ANGLES. IF YOU ARE RECORDING THE MOVEMENT OF A RIVER OF PEOPLE WALKING DOWN A WINDING PATH, TRY DIFFERENT ANGLES AND DISTANCES. IF YOU ARE RECORDING A LAKE, TRY TO SHOW THE ENTIRE LAKE THEN GET CLOSER SHOTS OF THE WAVES HITTING THE SHORE AND FISH IN THE SHALLOWS.

CHALLENGE YOURSELF. ON ONE VIDEO SAFARI, CONCENTRATE ON GETTING SHOTS OF JUST BIRDS. THE NEXT TIME, LOOK FOR SQUIRRELS, CHIPMUNKS, DEER, AND OTHER WILDLIFE. THEN ON ANOTHER DAY RECORD TREES AND FLOWERS AND MOVING WATER.

Project #6 - Moving Close Ups

Close up video is a great way to reveal a world people seldom appreciate. Instead of recording the vastness of a large park, explore a new universe by bringing your camera up close. Move the camera in and out of flowers in a flower bed to reveal the different colors and maybe an insect or two. Set up a village made of Legos and move the camera up close and around as if you were a little Lego person exploring your world. Use your imagination. You can find all kinds of "hidden" worlds just around your home.

 # IT'S A SMALL WORLD

RECORD THE INSECT WORLD. GET THE CAMERA DOWN TO AN INSECTS LEVEL AND RECORD ANTS, BEETLES, BUTTERFLIES AND MORE. BE CAREFUL OF STINGING BUGS

IF YOU HAVE A HOLIDAY TREE IN YOUR HOME HOLD YOUR SMARTPHONE CLOSE TO THE LIGHTS AND DECORATIONS AND SLOWLY MOVE YOUR CAMERA UP, DOWN AND AROUND THE TREE.

IF YOU HAVE A GARDEN, BRING THE SMARTPHONE CLOSE TO THE FLOWERS AND PLANTS AND SLOWLY MOVE THE CAMERA AROUND AND THROUGH THE PLANTS.

LINE UP A BUNCH OF YOUR TOYS ON THE FLOOR OR A TABLE AND MOVE THE SMART PHONE SLOWLY LEFT OR RIGHT.

IF YOU HAVE A TRAIN SET, PLACE THE CAMERA NEAR THE TRACK AND RECCORD THE TRAIN RUSHING BY.

FILL A TABLE WITH SMALL ITEMS FROM AROUND THE HOUSE. MOVE THE CAMERA IN AND OUT AROUND ALL THE ITEMS LIKE YOU ARE A MOUSE EXPLORING EVERY ITEMS.

A REAL, OUTSIDE TREE WOULD MAKE A GREAT SUBJECT FOR A MOVING ,O VIDEO. PLACE THE SMART PHONE CLOSE TO A TREE AND MOVE SLOWLY UPWARD.

Close Up Tips

When your subject is fuzzy and it's hard to make out details, then your camera is "out of focus". Try and keep the image looking sharp by backing up away from the subject.

Too close

Move camera back to focus

The Awesome Companion Book for Junior Movie Makers

Sometimes you can get a shadow from your hand or your body falling on the subject. To fix that problem try moving to a different angle or record using one hand and move the other hand out of the way.

Wait until the subject is in focus before recording. If possible use a mini tripod to record insects and other small wildlife. If you hold the camera, grip the smart phone firmly so it won't fall out of your hands.

Hold your camera level. Level means the camera is straight and flat instead of Look for a horizontal line, like the horizon or the top edge of a wall, to help you adjust the camera.

You can put the camera on a tripod and use a "level" app for proper adjustment. When the bubble appears in the center of the two lines, then the tripod is level.

Skits

Image from The Awesome Book of Home Movie Making.

On social media you can find thousands of examples of people posting videos of skits, music videos, movies, reviews and news stories. Making a movie, like the ones you see on TV, on-line or in the theater, requires a lot of preparation and can involve a lot of people. The best way to learn, however, is to start simply then create bigger and better videos as you learn.

The video skits in this book are designed as an introduction to making movies that tell a story using actors and sets. The skits have the basic elements of movie making: a description of the action, actors, dialogue between actors, and a graphic showing how to frame the action.

Moviemaking Tips

ADMIT ONE 405 163

SET THE CAMERA BACK FAR SO THAT EVERYONE INVOLVED IN THE SKIT CAN BE SEEN.

ADMIT ONE 405 163

MAKE SURE THAT THE SMART PHONE IS LEVEL AND NOT TILTED

ADMIT ONE 405 163

LOCK THE FOCUS OF YOUR SMART PHONE CAMERA BY PRESSING ON THE SCREEN WHERE YOU WANT TO FOCUS UNTIL AE/AF LOCK APPEARS. THAT WILL LOCK IN THE FOCUS

ADMIT ONE 405 163

TRY NOT TO RECORD THE SKIT IN FRONT OF A WINDOW ON A BRIGHT DAY. THE PEOPLE YOU ARE

ADMIT ONE 405 163

MAKE SURE THAT YOU CAN SEE EVERYONE IN THE SKIT AND YOU ARE NOT "CUTTING OFF THEIR HEADS" ON TOP OF THE SCREEN.

ADMIT ONE 405 163

MAKE SURE THE ACTORS SPEAK LOUDLY SO THE SMART PHONE CAN RECORD THEIR VOICES.

Skit #1 - Spider Scare

A young person (girl or boy) is sitting on a chair or a bench eating ice cream.

Suddenly, a spider creeps down from up above. When the kid sees the spider, he/she sets their ice cream on the chair and runs away.

After a short time, another person comes in holding a spider on a string and stick. The kid sits down and finishes the ice cream. The End

The Awesome Companion Book for Junior Movie Makers

Cast: Person #1 eating ice cream
Person #2 with spider

Setting: Inside in a kitchen or outside on a chair.

Person #1 is sitting down eating ice cream or pudding. He or she continues eating looking straight ahead as if watching TV. About ten seconds later Person #2 slowly lowers the fake spider down to Person #1's eye level .

At first Person #1 doesn't notice the spider but the he/she glances up, sees the spider and quickly sets down the ice cream on the chair and runs away out of the camera frame.

Person #2 walks into the frame still holding the spider on the string, grabs the ice cream and starts eating it.

Person #2 Says
"Ha, works every time."

Keep recording for 6 seconds and stop.

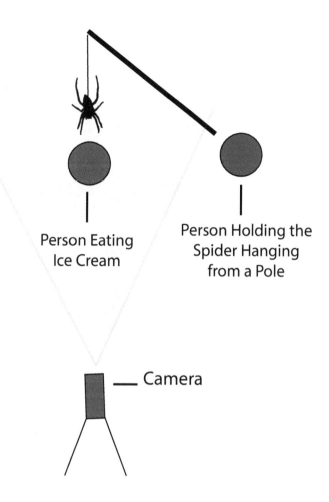

Keep the pole and the spider out of the camera's view then slowly lower the spider just in front of the person eating ice cream

If possible, tie the fake spider to the pole using a clear fishing line. The line will look like a spider web. Rubbing powder on the line will help reduce light reflection.

Wait at least 10 seconds before lowering the spider.

Use the link or scan the QR code below to download and print the spider.

https://www.retrorangerpub.com/spider

Image by Clker-Free-Vector-Images from Pixabay

Skit #2 - The Big "B"

In this story a person is sitting at a park bench.
Another person walks in and sits down beside the
first person, and they begin to talk.
The two of them start talking about insects.

Suddenly, the first person sees a big B and the
second person runs away.

Cast: Person #1 sitting on a bench
       Person #2 walks in and sits down

Setting: Outside bench at a park

The Awesome Companion Book for Junior Movie Makers

Person #1 is sitting down looking at a smartphone or reading a book. About 10 seconds later Person #2 comes in from the right of the frame and sits down next to Person #1.

Person #2 "Hey, what ca doing?"
Person #1 "Just reading this article about insects."
Person #2 "Yuk, I hate insects. They give me the creeps and some can sting you."
Person #1 "Actually, insects are very important for flowers and other plants."
Person #2 "Still, I wouldn't want one near me."
Person #1 (looking down at her feet) "Oh look, a big B."
Person #2 (jumps up and runs out of frame) "What! I'm outta here."
Person #1 (reaches down and grabs the letter B and holds it up.

Keep recording for about 6 seconds and stop.

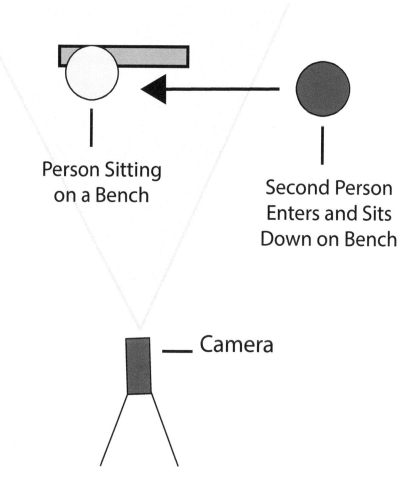

Person Sitting on a Bench

Second Person Enters and Sits Down on Bench

Camera

Cut out a big letter "B" out of cardboard or other stiff material.

Put the letter "B" on the ground beneath the first person sitting.

Set up the camera so the letter "B" can't be seen on screen.

When the person reaches down to pick up the "B", have them raise it up high enough for the camera to see.

Practice the skit several times before recording.

The Awesome Companion Book for Junior Movie Makers

Use the link or scan the QR code below to download and print a big letter "B".

https://www.retrorangerpub.com/big-b

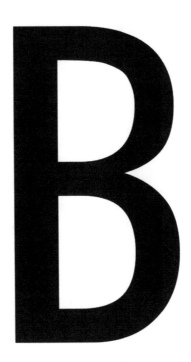

Glossary

Camera Lens - A part of the camera that focuses light to the camera sensor

Composition- how the subject is placed in the camera frame.

Dolly - moving the camera toward or away from your subject within a single shot.

Focus - to adjust an image so that it appears to be clear and sharp.

Frame – how the image fits in the camera screen.

Headroom - the space between the top of the subject and the top of the frame.

Interview - a discussion between two people with one person asking questions and the other answering questions.

Level - A flat or even surface compared to the ground.

Nose room - the space between the subject's nose and the edge of the frame.

Panning - A pan refers to the horizontal movement of the camera.

Shot - a single, nonstop operation of the video camera. When you start recording and then stop recording you've created a shot.

Smartphone - A mobile phone which contains a high quality camera.

Tracking Shot - Moving the camera alongside the action.

Tripod - a three-legged support for a camera or smart device.

The Awesome Companion Book for Junior Movie Makers

Mike Murphy

Mike Murphy has over forty years of experience in video and media production. He earned his BA in Communications from the University of Wisconsin-Parkside and an M Ed in Instructional Design and Technology from West Texas A&M.

Mike served as the media producer and photographer for several colleges. He is happily retired writing books, and continuing his hobbies in video and photography.

Mike currently resides in Kenosha, Wisconsin with his wife and fellow author, Gail.

Retro Ranger

Publishing Company

AWESOME
Companion Books

Hidden Hollow Tales

available at
amazon

Visit Our Website
www.retrorangerpub.com

Printed in the USA
CPSIA information can be obtained
at www.ICGtesting.com
LVHW071108041023
760113LV00017B/402